P9-EMF-408

*This book was a gift
to our library
from Capstone Press.*

LOSS

Understanding the Emptiness

WITHDRAWN

by Eileen Kuehn

Consultant:
Debbie Richey Stracener
Assistant Principal, Former Counselor
Greenwood High School
Bowling Green, Kentucky

LifeMatters
an imprint of Capstone Press
Mankato, Minnesota

LifeMatters Books are published by Capstone Press
PO Box 669 • 151 Good Counsel Drive • Mankato, Minnesota 56002
http://www.capstone-press.com

Printed in the United States of America

Library of Congress Cataloging-in-Publication Data
Kuehn, Eileen.
      Loss: understanding the emptiness / by Eileen Kuehn.
           p.   cm. — (Grief and loss)
      Includes bibliographical references and index.
      ISBN 0-7368-0746-2
      1. Loss (Psychology) in adolescence—Juvenile literature. 2. Grief in adolescence—Juvenile literature. [1. Loss (Psychology). 2. Grief.] I. Title. II. Series.
      BF724.3.L66 K84 2001
      155.9′3—dc21
                                         00-010922
                                         CIP

Summary: Defines loss and many ways in which it affects teens. Provides ideas to deal with loss in a helpful way, as well as tips to move beyond it and get on with life. Gives ways to help a friend deal with loss.

Staff Credits
Charles Pederson, editor; Adam Lazar, designer; Kim Danger, photo researcher

Photo Credits
Cover: UPmagazine/©Tim Yoon
©Artville/Simiji, 28
©DigitalVision/36
©RubberBall/45
Unicorn Stock Photos/©Jean Higgins, 19; ©Phyllis Kedl, 38; ©Aneal Vohra, 40; ©Eric R. Berndt, 46
Uniphoto Picture Agency/©Bob Daemmrich, 8, 27; ©Jackson Smith, 13; ©John Coletti, 22;
©Terry Way, 35
UPmagazine/©Tim Yoon, 59
Visuals Unlimited/©Cheryl A. Ertelt, 47; ©Jeff Greenberg, 57

A 0 9 8 7 6 5 4 3 2 1

Table of Contents

- Losses occur often in life. Some losses are major losses, such as the death of a loved one. Other losses are smaller and sometimes may not seem like losses until later.

- The loss of a relationship can be painful for a teen. He or she may have to face many other difficult losses.

- It's normal to feel sad and empty after a loss. It's also normal to feel that part of yourself has been lost.

- Loss forces change in life. It's easier to see the pattern of loss and change if you think about losses you've already experienced.

- Some cultures build an acceptance of loss into their beliefs.

Chapter 1

Introduction to Loss

Many Kinds of Loss

Life is filled with loss. When many people think of loss, they may think of someone's death. However, there are many losses. A library card is missing. A pet dies. A friend moves away. Parents divorce. Loss always includes disappointment. Anything that's difficult to handle can be a loss.

Loss may be thought of in two ways. First, it may be considered an event, either large or small. For example, the death of a grandparent is an event. Second, a loss may be considered more or less intense. The intensity is how painful the loss feels. The pain of a single event may be different for different people. A death is an intense loss. Divorce can be intense. Loss can be major if a relative becomes ill with Alzheimer's disease and no longer knows you. Alzheimer's affects a person's memory.

Losses happen every day. Some small losses may seem unimportant or may make you feel sad. For example, someone may yell at you for not taking out the garbage. Or you may overhear someone making fun of your clothes. These events can rob you of good feelings about yourself. If this happens, you may feel that you've lost the love and respect of another person, at least temporarily.

Every major loss makes a big impact on your life. These losses can affect you for a long time. Chapter 2 talks more about major loss. Other losses also can affect your life. These are discussed in Chapter 3.

Selena, Age 14

Selena, Twyla, and Roseanne were best friends throughout middle school. They laughed and cried together. They told each other their secrets, studied together, and hung out. They had looked forward to beginning 10th grade this year in high school.

One day, Twyla and Roseanne pretended not to see Selena. They turned and walked away whenever Selena approached. When Selena tried to sit with them at lunch, Twyla started to talk with someone next to her. Roseanne muttered, "That seat is saved."

Selena thought. "They really have dropped me. What happened?" She was miserable. Nothing made any sense. "Why won't they talk to me?" Selena's feelings seemed frozen. "What could happen to our friendship in one day? I feel empty inside," Selena sobbed to her mother. "I just don't understand why everything changed."

Loss Brings Emptiness

Selena seems to have lost her friends. The loss of a relationship like Selena's can be one of the most devastating changes a teen must live through. When a relationship ends, you usually feel sad and confused. You may feel like you're going crazy.

Did You Know?

An important book in China for thousands of years has been the *I Ching*, or the *Book of Changes*. Everyone from scholars to farmers has used it to understand changes in their life. The book explains that there are two opposing forces in life, called the yin and the yang. The *I Ching* teaches that one force always changes into the other. When yin influences a person's life for too long, it turns into its opposite—yang. This is a way of understanding how loss turns into change. Many people still read the *I Ching*.

Sadness may turn into anger and then blame. You might think it's your fault if the friend breaks off a relationship. You might wonder what you did wrong. You may start to think, "If only . . ." For example, "If only I hadn't told her how stupid she acts with her boyfriend."

After a relationship ends, the emptiness remains. You miss your friend and the good times you had together. Everything has changed. When Selena's friendships ended, she felt like there was a hole inside her.

Every loss can produce this emptiness. But every loss also can bring about the opportunity for something new. This new experience is called change.

Loss Makes Room for Change

Some adults think that the teen years are the happiest time of life. They forget that these years can be hard. They forget that teens go through many losses and many changes. Nothing is predictable for teens. They may feel like kids one day, and like adults the next. Just growing up can be a loss as teens leave childhood ways behind and become adults.

Change occurs when something happens to you. Change is the natural movement that takes place in life. It's normal for loss to force change. When a relationship ends, emptiness, intense pain, and sadness may remain. Then, as time passes, new activities and thoughts gradually fill the emptiness. With change can come growth. Even major losses can help people grow up and become more mature. Here are examples of what some people might consider a negative loss:

- Moving to a new city

- Breaking up with a boyfriend or girlfriend

- Having an older brother or sister move away from home

- Seeing parents get divorced

- Having a friend or close relative die

- Having a pet die

- Not making a team

- Having sex for the first time

- Having a parent lose a job, or losing a job oneself

- Discovering there really isn't a Santa Claus or tooth fairy

Loss and Culture

Some experts who study culture believe North American teens aren't well prepared to adjust to loss and change. There's still a myth in this culture that people are meant to live happily ever after. We think that loss will never happen to us. We may think that if we have to experience loss, it will be far in the future. Sometimes we prefer to think that loss happens only to other people.

However, loss can bring growth when it's properly accepted. Some cultures have built an acceptance of loss and change into their beliefs. This may be a ritual or ceremony to celebrate a special occasion called a rite of passage. For example, some American Indian boys perform a ceremony of bravery to mark the time they become men. Jewish boys and girls might celebrate a bar mitzvah and bat mitzvah when they reach the age of 13. This signals that they have become adults.

Points to Consider

o How might divorce be considered negative loss? How might it be positive?

o How would you feel if you had to move to a new city? Explain.

o Do you have any celebrations for rites of passage? If so, explain. If not, do you think such celebrations would be helpful in dealing with loss? Why or why not?

- When a loss is expected, you may be able to prepare for it. When the loss happens suddenly, you may feel that there's no time to prepare. Still, there are ways to prepare for even sudden loss.

- Survivors of a death have many questions. Their feelings may be confused.

- Shock is usually the first reaction to a major loss. Later, people may feel guilt, blame, fear, longing, or sadness about it.

- A person goes through three grieving phases during a major loss: avoidance, confrontation, and accommodation.

Chapter 2

Major Loss

A major loss can be anything that causes intense pain and sadness. It may be the split of a family through divorce. It could be the loss of a pet or a breakup with a girlfriend or boyfriend. It could be anything that feels major to you, even if other people don't think so.

Major loss happens to everyone at some time. You might think that there's no way to prepare for it. However, just accepting that loss will occur can help you prepare. Whether a loss is expected or sudden may make a difference in how you react, too. You can't choose your feelings, but you can choose how to react to them.

Teen Talk

"When my cat ran away, I cried and cried for days. I'm sure people thought it was crazy for a guy to cry about a cat. But that cat was my best friend. She eventually came back, but man, that was a bad time."—Paul, age 15

Expected Loss

When loss is expected, accepting it might be easier. There's time to adjust to the idea of the loss beforehand. For instance, you might know you're going to move or get a bad grade in a class. You can prepare yourself for the feelings that may come with those losses.

For teens, the death of a loved one is one of the most stressful of all life's losses. It may be the first experience with a major loss. However, you may have known for some time that the person will die. This can give you time to be with the loved one and say good-bye. Sometimes this makes the loss more bearable.

Accepting a loss may be easier if you can prepare for it.
For example, you may know you'll get a bad grade.
Then you can get ready for the feelings it may bring.

Sudden Loss

Luis, Age 15

Luis was waiting for his friend Wong all evening. They planned to study together, but Wong didn't come. Luis began to get angry. "The least he could do is call," he told his mother. "There's no way I'm studying with him anymore!"

The next morning Luis heard that Wong was killed in a drive-by shooting. He'd been biking to Luis's house as a car raced past. Several shots came from the open car windows. Wong fell from his bike and ended up dying because of massive bleeding.

Luis couldn't believe it at first. Then, he realized that while Wong was bleeding, Luis was blaming him for not keeping the study date. "I should have been on that bike," Luis said. "I'm the one who should be shot."

The leading cause of death for people ages 10 to 24 is motor vehicle accidents. The second and third leading causes of death among people ages 15 to 24 are murder and killing themselves.

A fatal automobile accident snatches away life in an instant. A heart attack or a stroke may cause immediate death. Survivors, or those left behind after a death, have no time to be with their loved one before death. They have no chance to say good-bye. The emotions of a sudden loss are usually different from those of an expected loss. For example, Luis blames himself for what happened to Wong. Yet, clearly Luis could have done nothing to prevent the shooting.

Painful Questions

When a loved one dies suddenly, survivors are left with many painful questions. Why did she kill herself? Why was he shot down in the street? What caused the accident?

All of these confused thoughts are layered over sadness. Survivors also may have to deal with their own feelings of guilt and blame.

Shock

It's normal to go into a state of disbelief when a major loss occurs. This state is called shock. It is usually the first reaction to a major loss. Sometimes everything becomes a blur after the news of a major loss. It may be hard to do anything. You may feel paralyzed. Nothing seems to make any sense.

Shock also can produce many other feelings. Guilt, blame, fear, longing, and sadness all can be mixed up like the ingredients in a salad. You might even experience all of these feelings at once.

Shock is the body's way of getting used to bad news slowly. During shock, the body lets only a little pain come through at one time. A person in shock may feel like he or she is walking around in someone else's body.

People react to a major loss in different ways. Some people scream and cry. Others are icy calm. They might get busy with details so they don't have to think. Only later, sometimes days, months, or years later, will some people let their pain out. Take a look at Jerry's reaction to a loss.

Jerry, Age 16

"Lila Victor, age 60, died of complications from cancer," the newspaper read. Jerry couldn't believe it. He'd delivered groceries to Mrs. Victor only two weeks ago. She'd been watching TV and had looked fine to him then.

Mrs. Victor had lived alone in an apartment down the block. Jerry had been about 6 years old the first time he met her. He'd been riding his bike in front of Mrs. Victor's building when he fell and cut his knee. Mrs. Victor came off the stoop and carried him into her apartment. She cleaned and gently bandaged his knee, then walked him and his bike home.

Over the years, they became good friends. She always had time to listen to Jerry's problems. Sometimes, he'd help her around the apartment or get her groceries. Now she was gone. He missed her already. He hadn't even known she was sick. "She's too great a person to just die like that. Maybe this is all a dream," Jerry thought. But it wasn't.

Jerry and his parents went to Mrs. Victor's funeral. That was when her death hit him. He had to get out of there or he'd scream. Jerry slipped out and found a hidden area in the children's playground. The sobs seemed to tear his body apart. He hit the earth with his fists. It was so unfair! Why did she die? Jerry couldn't find any answers. He just cried until there were no more tears.

Grieving

After the initial shock from a major loss passes, you must look for ways to deal with your pain. This is what happened to Jerry after he worked through his initial shock. You can expect the feelings of loss, sadness, and emptiness to continue for a long time. These feelings are grouped together into an emotion called grief, which occurs after any major loss. The process of feeling and dealing with grief can be called grieving.

A person goes through three phases of grieving during a major loss. Each phase marks the point where you are in the grieving process. The three phases are avoidance, confrontation, and accommodation.

Avoidance

The first phase of grieving is avoidance. It's when you avoid the truth. You may try to pretend the loss didn't happen. You might hope the loss was a bad dream. At first, Jerry couldn't bring himself to believe that Mrs. Victor was gone. He didn't want to face his feelings.

During the avoidance phase, you may not be able to understand what happened. You may feel confused and keep asking why. At this time it's normal to want answers about why the loss occurred. This is especially true if the loss was sudden.

Teen Talk

"After my best friend got arrested for drunk driving, I blamed myself for a long time. I mean, I was at the same party as she was and I could have stopped her from driving."—Patty, age 17

Confrontation

The second phase of grief is confrontation. In this phase, people come face to face with their loss. This is when you accept that the loss happened. Usually this doesn't make the pain easier to bear. In fact, this can be when you feel the most pain. Jerry began to confront his grief about Mrs. Victor's death at her funeral. He felt torn apart by his grief.

You know you can't go back to the time before the loss. But a part of you still may want to go back. Imagine you go to the door to call your dog. Then the truth hits you. Your dog was hit by a car and died. Never again will you be able to play with your pet. People have described this sharp, sudden feeling as a pang of grief.

Although painful, a pang of grief may help you confront the reality of the loss. Each time it happens, you take another step forward in working through your grief. By recognizing his feelings, Jerry began the process of learning to live with his emotions.

During the confrontation phase of grief, you may have many confusing emotions. You may experience unexplained anger. You may feel abandoned, become afraid, or feel sad. You might feel all of these at once. Crazy feelings come when you least expect them.

Accommodation

The third phase of grieving is accommodation. This is a gradual acceptance of loss on a daily basis. The pangs of grief become less painful. When this happens, you know you're beginning to get beyond the loss. Little by little, you begin to feel more able to go on. Life can't go back to the way it was before, but you can learn to handle the loss.

Accommodation is a slow process. This phase of grieving can take years. It's the healing that takes place as you work through your feelings of loss. As Jerry reached the accommodation phase, he got help from many sources such as his mother and friends. Working through grief is discussed more in Chapter 4.

Points to Consider

- What would you say to a loved one who is facing death?

- Have you ever experienced a major loss? How did you feel?

- What do you think creates the feeling of emptiness that many survivors of major loss talk about?

○ Hundreds of losses happen to people in their lifetime. Even though these losses may not be major, they are still painful.

○ Like major losses, smaller losses affect people in different ways. A person may have strong grief feelings connected with loss.

○ North American culture gives tough messages about handling loss. These cultural messages may discourage healing from the grief of a loss.

○ Loss may affect a person's self-esteem. Loss also can contribute to post-traumatic stress disorder.

○ It's important to recognize and work through the feelings of loss. People who ignore feelings of loss may develop serious problems later in life.

Loss

Other Losses

Other Kinds of Loss

When people talk about loss, they often mean major losses. Some of these were discussed in Chapter 2. But hundreds of smaller losses also happen. These smaller losses may not always seem important, but they still may be hard on you.

Moving to a new city can be a loss. So can changing schools, losing a pet, or breaking up with someone. It's a loss when you don't get the lead in the class play that you had hoped for. Physical, emotional, or mental abuse can create loss. A disappointing test score is a loss. Look at the following two examples of different kinds of loss.

Keesha and Mike, Ages 17 and 16

Keesha and Mike's home was put up for sale. They had lived in that house their whole life. Keesha and Mike tried to talk their parents into waiting a year and a half to move. They wanted to finish high school in their hometown.

Keesha and Mike's parents wouldn't change their minds. The move to a new city was definite. "No, the time to go is now," Keesha's father told them. "I want a new job in a warmer climate. If I wait much longer, I'll be too old to get a good job."

Keesha was angry. "We don't count for anything," she told Mike. "Dad and Mom don't care about our feelings."

Keesha quit talking to her parents after the decision to move. "Why should I?" she said angrily. "They think we're dirt, anyway."

Loss

Some people who grieve a loss may feel open to religious experiences more than before the loss. On the other hand, many people feel angry at their god or supreme being.

Larry, Age 15

Larry and his father had found Larry's dog, Bear, when Larry was 9. Bear slept at the foot of Larry's bed every night. They took long runs together. Bear listened with a serious face when Larry played his CDs. She seemed to want to comfort Larry when he had problems.

One day when Larry came home from school, Bear was gone. Larry looked for days all around the neighborhood and put up signs everywhere. No one responded.

After two months, Larry still hadn't found Bear. Larry couldn't concentrate on school. He didn't feel like eating. All he could think about was Bear. Was she dead or alive? Did someone steal her? His parents told him to get on with his life. Larry couldn't stand it when they said that. "You don't know what it's like to lose your best friend," he shouted.

Teen Talk

"The other night, I couldn't sleep, so I went downstairs to get some milk. As I was walking to the fridge, I saw my mom kissing her new boyfriend. She's single, and it's her life, so whatever. But it bugs me. I feel like I'm losing her."—Kyle, age 14

Loss Is Personal

Loss is different for everyone. What seems like a huge loss to you may not seem like a loss at all to someone else. What's important is how *you* feel about the loss. For this reason, it's not always possible to compare losses among people. Losses affect different people in different ways. Even if they don't bother you too much, small losses still may create a feeling of disappointment and emptiness.

There's no right or wrong way to feel about loss. It's normal to feel sad, lonely, confused, angry, afraid, or crabby when you lose something. You also may feel disappointed, tired, guilty, worried, helpless, or resentful. These feelings can be strong and obvious. At other times, they can be hard to detect. The feelings may come and go. For example, you may find yourself laughing loudly about something that isn't even funny. A minute later you may blow up in a temper tantrum or cry for no reason.

Grief Feelings

The feelings that come with loss are feelings of grief. You may avoid grief for a while. However, there's no way to stop it permanently. Grieving is the process of learning how to work through the grief feelings of loss.

Since many people ignore or don't talk much about smaller losses, they may not realize they're grieving. Here are some signs of unhealthy grieving from losses.

- Making mistakes

- Having low energy, lack of motivation, or lack of interest in normal activities

- Having a negative outlook on life

- Feeling embarrassed, unsure, hopeless, sad, or desperate

- Changing moods quickly

- Having nightmares

- Lacking concentration or the ability to think of anything but the loss

- Having loss of appetite or else eating all the time

- Being suddenly angry at people, your god, or the universe

These symptoms of grieving are the mental, emotional, physical, and spiritual expressions of pain. If you have some of the symptoms on this list, you may be grieving. You may want to see a doctor or counselor for help in working through your grief.

Teen Talk

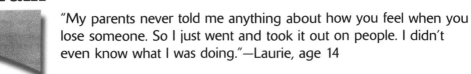

Avoiding Grief Feelings

Some people may do anything to distract themselves from their grief. They might pretend that the loss isn't important. They may use alcohol and other drugs or watch TV constantly. They might try to hurt themselves or others.

Adults may teach kids to put on a tough show about loss. For example, imagine your pet dies. Your parents may say, "It's just a dog." "Fluffy was old and lived a good life." "Grow up." "Stop crying." "Put it behind you." You might learn that it's not okay to express feelings of sadness and grief.

Some cultures give tough messages about handling loss. For example, many North Americans are expected to handle their problems alone and get over loss quickly. How often have you heard someone say "Deal with it" or "Take it like an adult"? These messages about loss are deep within much of U.S. and Canadian culture.

Feelings may become too hard to deal with. Some people may refuse even to acknowledge that they have feelings. In this way, they try to avoid the pain and hurt of more losses. However, people need to learn to face and work through these feelings in order to heal.

Loss

Self-Esteem Can Be Affected

One result of avoiding grief feelings is that you might feel worthless. This feeling is called a lack of self-esteem, or the value you place on yourself.

Not recognizing or avoiding feelings of loss can cause feelings of hopelessness to develop. You might not feel good about yourself. Low self-esteem like this robs a person of a sense of worth. It's like a downward spiral that sometimes turns into depression. Hopelessness and depression can make everything seem pointless.

A loss may be major or minor, but each loss brings change. If the loss is expressed through healthy grieving, you can go on to healthier things. If the loss isn't expressed, many problems can result.

The Effects of Loss

Some people have had lots of loss in their life. They may have come to expect or gotten used to disappointment. They may believe nothing good ever happens to them.

As you get older, you collect more memories of losses. This can help you handle smaller losses more calmly. However, sometimes the losses blur together. This may create a deep sadness. You may not express feelings of loss, but you still may be hurting and in deep pain.

Some people live in constant fear of loss from violence and death. They may become serious, sad people who are cut off from their feelings. They may not be able to be playful, creative, or open to love. They may seem to be uncaring about other people or about life.

Post-Traumatic Stress Disorder

Sometimes people get used to living with violence in their home and community. Even if a person gets away from a violent environment, the hidden feelings may come back later in life. This is called post-traumatic stress disorder (PTSD).

Post-traumatic stress disorder sometimes happens to soldiers who have been at war. It also is recognized sometimes in people who grow up with lots of loss in their life. It can occur to people in neighborhoods in which violence often occurs.

People with PTSD may get angry for no reason or have fears and nightmares. They may act inappropriately or become depressed. When enough anger gets hidden inside, people may become like a bomb waiting to explode. Such people may commit random acts of violence because of PTSD.

Dealing With Loss

You might choose to deal with a loss as it happens. Or, you might push it out of your mind and try to forget it. Sometimes it seems like not thinking about a loss is the easiest thing.

This isn't necessarily true. Over time, losses add up. If you avoid painful feelings about loss, they may seem to disappear. However, they still are somewhere inside you, even if you don't recognize them. It may take special counseling to understand these deep, hidden feelings. For example, many teens may have experienced losses but didn't have help to work through the feelings. Seeing a professional counselor can be helpful for these students.

Teen Talk

The way people deal with loss and grieving usually comes from their background. Children and teens often learn to handle their feelings the way they see people around them handle theirs. People who don't learn helpful ways to deal with loss feelings may set themselves up for problems later in life. Learning to grieve losses in positive, helpful ways can help people throughout their life. It can help people to become stronger individuals.

Points to Consider

- Do you think it's okay to pretend you feel fine when you don't feel that way? Explain.

- Have you ever noticed someone's self-esteem affected by a loss? If so, how did that person change?

- Have you or anyone you know ever hidden your feelings to avoid the pain of a loss? If so, what happened?

- How do you feel about handling loss "like an adult"?

Chapter Overview

- If you don't let go of or accept loss, it may become hidden. Feelings that go with loss may become stronger until they're dealt with.

- You can't run away from feelings of loss. Don't push yourself to feel better quickly when you've had a loss. Working through grief takes time.

- Grief work can help you heal the sadness in your mind, body, and soul. Uncovering buried feelings of loss can be done as part of your grief work.

Chapter 4

Growing Beyond Loss

Letting Go

The words *letting go* often are used in connection with grieving. If you can't let go of or accept a loss, it may become buried inside you. Letting go is necessary in healthy grieving. It's one of the most important things you can do to begin your healing from loss. Letting go of the memory of a loss opens space for changes in life.

Mayla, Age 17

Mayla's grandmother died after a two-year struggle with cancer. Mayla had spent a lot of time in the hospital. Her grandmother said it was okay for Mayla to cry. Mayla's grandmother discussed many feelings about death, so Mayla thought she knew what to expect. Mayla was prepared for the death.

Now Mayla was confused. She knew she was grieving the death of her grandmother. But she also thought a lot about her father. When Mayla was 5, her father left the family. He never came back or even called.

Although Mayla knew about feelings of loss, she felt as helpless now as when her father abandoned her. She wanted her father back. She remembered how lost and alone she'd felt. She felt all the insecurity and confusion of a 5-year-old whose parent had walked out on her.

Finally, she couldn't stand it any longer. She made an appointment to talk with a loss counselor about her confused feelings. The counselor explained that her grandmother's death had triggered the memories of her father. The emotions Mayla felt when she was 5 had become hidden. Mayla had never worked through that early loss, the counselor told her. No one had helped her.

The loss of her grandmother had brought back those old feelings. Now, with help, Mayla was grieving her father as she couldn't when she was 5.

A loss that hasn't been dealt with may seem to be gone, but it isn't. Mayla's grandmother's death was a gift. She helped Mayla understand her loss feelings when a loved one dies. Through it, Mayla was able to open up long-buried childhood feelings of loss. Finally, she could productively grieve her father's long-ago abandonment.

You Can't Run From Loss

The better we learn to handle loss, the healthier and happier we'll be. Handling loss begins with facing the loss as a normal part of life. Healthy grieving helps us face the sadness and pain of any loss.

As you grow beyond feelings of loss, it's important not to push yourself to feel better quickly. Because you feel pain during loss, you may want to run away or do something dramatically different.

However, don't begin or end a relationship, buy an expensive item, use alcohol or other drugs, or quit school. These changes create only temporary distractions from the pain of loss. Try not to make big decisions within the first six months to a year following a major loss. Big decisions at this time can create too much change and distract you from healthy grieving. As painful as it is, it's better to work through—not avoid—your feelings of loss.

While you're working through a loss, it's important to take good care of your body. You need healthy food and exercise to keep your energy flowing. Drink lots of water. Get some sleep instead of spending hours in front of the TV or computer screen.

Grief Work

Having a healthy body will help you begin to deal with grief and its emotions. This is called grief work, which is a process for working through loss. Grief work can bring about healing and the opportunity to experience positive change. The empty holes that loss leaves gradually are filled with new, more useful things.

Set aside special time every day to rest and do grief work. It's important not to build walls around yourself. Take time to be alone but don't isolate yourself from others. Balance your quiet time with social activities.

Remember that working through grief needs to be done at your own pace. The time you need is yours alone and will probably be different from the time other people need. Most people haven't had much training in doing grief work. You need private time to recognize and work through your feelings of loss.

Research shows that intense grieving can last as long as a year. Some people may need as long as two years to work through their intense grief.

While working on your grief, try to keep your life as simple as possible. Don't take on new responsibilities. Keep your daily schedule easy. Don't try to keep everything the way it was before the loss. Feeling confused as your life changes is part of the grieving process. Keeping things simple should lessen the confusion.

Uncovering Buried Feelings of Loss

Losses gradually add up over time. It's important not to cover up loss and hurting. Don't deny your emotions. Some people deny feelings of loss by concentrating on passive activities such as watching TV. As Mayla did, we also need to learn how to deal with buried losses. This may be done with the help of a counselor. Or you may want to make it part of your grief work. Many tools can help do that. Some examples follow.

Reflections in a Pool

Rituals can be helpful in releasing the pain of loss. For this personal ritual, find a place to relax. Take slow, deep breaths. Picture a pond or pool on a warm summer day. Listen to the sounds around the pool, whether that's birds, people's voices, or passing cars. Smell the flowers growing at the edge of the pool. Feel the warm sand or cement under your feet.

Continue to take deep, relaxing breaths. Imagine that you're bending over and looking into the water. See your own face mirrored there. Notice the changes in your face. Think about the memories and feelings behind your face.

Every now and then, imagine you touch the water with your hand. Speak to the part of you that's holding on to loss and grief. Imagine yourself sprinkling the water over yourself as you say, "I release myself from this pain." Do this several times.

Imagine the pain of long-buried loss leaving your body. Breathe deeply and feel your body release the pain. Tell yourself you're ready for joy to come into your body. Imagine joy filling the space where the pain was.

When your ritual is complete, open your eyes. Take with you the memory of being free from pain.

Keep a Journal

Before healing can begin, you need to recognize what is causing the pain. Writing about your feelings in a journal is a good way to begin the healing process. As a part of your grief work, commit yourself to write for 15 to 20 minutes every day.

The journal can help you sort out your feelings. Write what you think and feel. You may feel relief when you put the hurt, anger, confusion, or pain down on paper. Once you've written down your thoughts, they may lose their intensity. They also may lose their power to stay in your mind.

Personal Loss History

Understanding loss can be easier if you examine the losses you've already experienced. You can do this with a personal loss history.

Divide a sheet of paper into three parts. Label one part *Major or Minor Loss*, the middle part *Loss Event*, and the last part *Change After Loss*.

In the middle column, write down losses you've experienced. Then, in the left column, write whether it was a major or minor loss. In the right column, write down a change that came from the loss. There may be more than one change. List all the changes that you can think of for each event, positive or negative. Your personal loss history can help you see how your life has changed.

Other Grief Work

Some other helpful ways of working through grief can include the following:

- Listen to music.

- Act out your feelings in a private place. Pound or scream into a pillow. Have a temper tantrum on your bed or a mattress.

- Join an art or poetry therapy class.

- Read.

- Exercise.

- Do kind things for others.

- Meditate.

- Find a friend who has experienced a similar loss.

- Have fun.

It's important not to hurry through the grieving process. Grief work may take more time for some people, less time for others. An expert on grieving once said: "It takes as long as it takes."

Points to Consider

- Can you remember a loss you experienced as a child? Did you learn anything about the loss?

- Why do you think it might help to write down your sad and painful feelings about a loss?

- Can you think of helpful ways to express anger or sadness about a loss? What are they?

- Have you ever pretended a loss wasn't important to you? What do you feel about it now when you think about it?

- High self-esteem can help you get through loss. Teens with low self-esteem may find it difficult to stay on the healing path.

- You can oppose negative self-talk by giving yourself positive messages.

- Finding your healing path allows you to manage the painful feelings from loss. Still, feelings from loss can return years after a loss.

- Physical symptoms of unhealthy grieving must be recognized. These symptoms happen because of the stress of loss and grief.

- There are many ways to get help when you're grieving a loss. These include support groups and counseling.

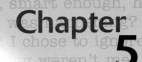
The Healing Path

Elyse, Age 14

Elyse had gone to seven schools by the time she was in the sixth grade. Her parents thought new experiences were good for her. Elyse knew better.

"I was always the new face," she told her loss support group. "The teacher and students always called me that. I didn't have a name. It always made me feel that I was on the outside, looking in. I was always alone in a different world. No one respected me. I laugh now when people talk about low self-esteem. My problem wasn't low self-esteem. It was no self-esteem."

Teen Talk

"My little brother always got D's in math. I laughed at him and called him stupid because all my grades were high. I wonder if he killed himself because of that."—Bob, age 16

Loss of Self

Elyse felt ignored. This was a loss of part of herself. The most personal loss you can experience is losing your sense of self-esteem.

Comments by others can take away our feelings of self-esteem. When we feel something is wrong with us, criticism can be damaging. Failure may add to our feeling of being worth less than others. Frequent disappointments also can chip away at our feelings of self-worth. Each disappointment may seem small when looked at by itself. But when one small loss is piled on many others, all our value may feel stripped away.

Self-esteem or the lack of it affects all of a person's thoughts and actions. Teens with low self-esteem may find it difficult to stay on the healing path. Strong self-esteem can help you get through loss in a more secure way.

Opposing Negative Self-Talk

Fortunately, tools are available to help us restore lost self-esteem. One of them is to use positive self-talk. You may tell yourself, "I might as well give up." Eventually, you may begin to believe the negative messages.

The next time you give yourself negative messages, talk back to yourself. Say "Stop it" to the voice. Then begin to use positive messages instead of negative ones. Tell yourself, "I am a good person." "I deserve to feel good about myself." "I'm not going to give up." "I can make a difference."

Do this each time negative thoughts pop up. After a while, it may be easier to shut off your negative voice. As you begin to feel better about yourself, that negative voice should fade away. Your self-esteem can increase, and you may find that you're no longer so open to smaller losses.

Finding Your Healing Path

Healing a loss is like going on a hike. You need the proper gear, patience, and strength. On a hike, it's important not to do things too quickly. If you hike too fast, you'll wear yourself out. You also won't have time to enjoy things along the way. Going fast isn't always the healthiest thing to do.

As you travel your healing path, you also must allow the painful feelings of loss to heal. They may never disappear, but you can learn to live with them. It's important to look at all the different paths to make sure you take the best one for you.

Feelings From Loss Can Return

Healing a loss isn't a one-time thing. This may be due to your growing maturity. As people get older, they might be able to handle things in a different, often better, way than before. This may make it necessary to deal with feelings from loss again.

Years after you think you've gotten over a loss, the pain may return. You may see a dog like the one you lost years ago, and you feel sharp, confrontational grief again. An old girlfriend or boyfriend may walk toward you on the street. The pain of the breakup years ago may be suddenly fresh in your mind.

Remembering losses is normal and healthy. You can expect to remember losses from various times. Each time you remember a loss, you will deal with it a little differently. Each time you deal with it, you'll learn something new about yourself.

You might consider these feelings as refresher courses in your grief work. When these reminders come, you may have to backtrack and reexamine the healing path you chose. Every time you redo your grief work, you can make yourself stronger.

In grief work, the goal is to remain patient while the natural healing process runs its course. However, sometimes people can get stuck in their grief. When this happens, it's easy to move into grieving that isn't productive or useful.

Teen Talk

"When I go to my loss support group I don't feel alone. I see people who have had the same type of loss that I had. They seem to have come out of it okay."—Mary Kay, age 15

Unhelpful Grieving

In nonproductive grieving, the body, mind, and soul can become sick. When too many bad feelings are ignored, the body often will react.

Sometimes the reaction may be a headache. Other times you may get a stomachache or a cold. If the grief isn't released, over time the body may develop a more serious disease. Unreleased grief can result in stress, which is linked to heart disease and high blood pressure. It also may play a part in causing cancer.

In learning about helpful ways to work through loss, it's important to recognize physical symptoms of unhelpful grieving. Chapter 3 mentioned some of these symptoms.

Support Systems

Sometimes it's difficult to do grief work alone. If you need help, friends and family can be natural support systems. Parents can be the most helpful. Schools often have counselors and social workers who can help you understand loss and grief. Sometimes talking with a favorite teacher, coach, or spiritual leader can help put you on the path to healing.

Don't rule out the relief you can get from attending a loss support group or from counseling. When you're in pain, you may need someone who is trained to help you work through your grief.

Support Groups

Loss support groups can be an important source of help. There are many benefits from sharing your feelings with people who have similar feelings. Just knowing you're not alone in your feelings can be a big help.

There are a number of ways to find such a group. One is to see the For More Information section on pages 60 and 61. Ask the resources listed there for a referral to a local loss support group. You also can call a local crisis telephone line or teen hot line.

Counseling

If you want to talk with a trained professional, ask someone you trust for some names. Ask for a referral from parents, school counselors, teachers, doctors, clergy, or other adults. Ask someone at one of the phone numbers on page 60. Maybe you know someone who sees a counselor. Ask if that person respects and likes the counselor. If so, you might go to that counselor for help. If you have the chance, you might want to find out beforehand:

o Does the counselor work a lot with teens?

o How does the counselor feel about personal loss?

o What kind of advice, if any, does the counselor give teens?

If you talk with the counselor, ask yourself these questions about your conversation:

o Did you feel the counselor really listened to you?

o Did you feel comfortable or anxious when you had your first talk with the counselor? If you were anxious, decide if you want to find a different counselor.

o Did the counselor seem to accept you for who you are? Or did you feel he or she would try to change you?

Did You Know?

Loss support groups and organizations can help give teens a safe place to express feelings. These groups can:

- Help young people understand grief-related feelings such as anger and denial
- Help young people with their grief work
- Improve family relationships
- Be a source for new friends

Organizations That Can Help

Many organizations can help young people deal with loss. These organizations may offer private advice and referrals to other helpful sources. Check the For More Information section starting on page 60.

Points to Consider

- Did the feelings from an old loss ever return later? How did you deal with the feelings?

- Have you ever wanted help in dealing with a loss? What happened?

- Have you ever felt any of the physical symptoms that could mean stress from loss? How did you deal with those symptoms? Was your way helpful?

Chapter Overview

- There are many ways to help people who are grieving.

- Being an active listener is one of the best ways to help a friend who is experiencing loss. An active listener must have empathy and the ability to be a word detective.

- A journal is a good gift for someone who is grieving. Writing is a good way to uncover your true feelings.

- Suggest that a grieving friend join a loss support group. Offer to go with him or her. By supporting your friend, you may help yourself grow as a person.

Chapter 6

Helping Others Deal With Loss

Jamal and Tom, Age 15

Jamal's friend Tom said he and his family were moving out of their house into an apartment. Tom's father lost his job. He'd been trying to find another one but with no luck. Tom mentioned adjustments he and his family were forced to make. No new computer. No more cool clothes. Getting rid of the family's new car. "Dad also told me to forget about college. There goes my future!"

Tom stopped talking. He was trying not to cry. "Go ahead and cry," Jamal said, "It helps release some of the pressure you're under." When Tom could listen again, Jamal said, "I know it's going to be tough for a while, but you're resourceful. I know you can make things work out."

"That's easy for you to say," Tom growled. "It's not your life that just went down the tube!" Jamal didn't respond to the rude remark. "What am I going to do?" Tom said. "There's nothing to live for."

"You have almost two years to save up for college," Jamal told Tom. "It's not too early to start applying for financial aid. Maybe you can get a scholarship."

Tom said, "I suppose that's true. And I don't think it'd be hard to get a part-time job at the grocery store. Thanks, Jamal."

At a Glance

It took courage for Jamal to stick by Tom. Being a good friend to someone during a time of loss requires a lot of understanding. People grieving a loss often feel totally confused, powerless, and helpless. Your friend may resent you for trying to help. However, your friend hurts a lot and may not even be aware of being rude or resentful. Be willing to overlook rudeness or mean remarks.

Suggestions for Helping a Friend Deal With Loss

There are ways to help someone who is grieving a loss. Here are some things to remember:

o Be available when your friend needs you.

o Don't give any advice unless your friend asks for it.

o Help your friend recover from grief one day at a time.

o If your friend seems depressed, tell parents, a teacher, a spiritual leader, or other trusted adult. You aren't telling on your friend. You'll be helping him or her.

o Know when to leave your friend alone.

"At first, I was really hurt when my friend snapped at me. I was just trying to help. Then I realized she was dealing with her loss. It still hurts a little, but at least I know she didn't mean to be rude."
—Grace, age 15

- No one can grieve in your friend's place. But you might help just by being there.

- Tell your friend that the grief lessens after a while. Encourage your friend to stay hopeful until it does.

- Help your friend take small steps into the future.

Listen Actively

One big skill that Jamal practiced was being an active listener as Tom talked about his loss. Jamal knows that active listening is an important part of helping a friend through the grieving process. Having empathy and being a word detective are two ways to help you be an active listener.

Empathy is the ability to feel someone else's feelings. Let's say your friend is sad about a poor grade. Think of a time you were in a similar situation. When you remember your feelings in that situation, you might be able to know what your friend feels, too. When people grieve, they may not want advice but just a friendly listener. It may help them just to know that someone understands them.

A word detective hunts for clues about what the friend is really feeling. There are three ways to do this.

First, listen to what your friend does say. Don't think about what you want to say next. Concentrate only on your friend's words.

Second, listen to what your friend doesn't say. For example, maybe your friend's parents just divorced. You might expect this to be the first thing your friend wants to talk about. Instead, maybe she or he starts talking about a local sports team. This might be a clue that your friend is avoiding the feelings about the divorce.

Finally, listen for the words your friend uses. These words can point to feelings. For example, your friend may say: "I have nothing to live for." In reality, your friend may be thinking about killing himself or herself.

Give a Gift Journal

A good gift for a grieving friend is a blank book or notebook. It's a place for your friend to write his or her feelings. Explain that journals are private and no one else will read what your friend writes. Tell your friend that the writing is only for him or her and doesn't have to be perfect. Writing can help your friend discover hidden feelings. Here are some other suggestions you could give your friend about writing in a journal:

- Set aside time when you won't be interrupted.

- If you can't get started, try beginning a sentence with: "I'm remembering . . ." Do this whenever you get stuck.

- You may want to write down your dreams.

- For 10 or 15 minutes, write anything that comes to mind. Just keep writing without lifting the pen from the page. Don't read anything you write until the time is up.

Support Groups

You may want to suggest that your friend join a teen loss support group. The people in a support group share similar feelings. Talking about things in a group can help the healing. You might offer to go to the first meeting with your friend.

A Special Friend

It takes a special friend to help another person through the grieving process. It can be difficult and may almost break the friendship. It also can strengthen the friendship. And helping a friend who is grieving a loss can help you grow as a person.

Points to Consider

- Do you think you would find it difficult to talk with a grieving friend? Why or why not?

- Do you consider yourself an active listener? Explain.

- How do you think you could help a friend who is grieving?

- Would you feel comfortable suggesting a teen loss support group for your grieving friend? Would you go with him or her? Explain.

Note

At publication, all resources listed here were accurate and appropriate to the topics covered in this book. Addresses and phone numbers may change. When visiting Internet sites and links, use good judgment. Remember, never give personal information over the Internet.

Internet Sites

Counseling for Loss and Life Changes
www.counselingforloss.com
Links to other grief-related Internet sites

Death and Dying
www.death-dying.com/teen.html
Articles and a special chat rooms for teens

SA\VE Suicide Awareness Voices of Education
www.save.org
Online grief and outreach support group for survivors of suicide and others

Hot Lines

Boy's Town Hot Line
1-800-448-3000

National AIDS Hot Line
1-800-342-AIDS (1-800-342-2437)

Youth Crisis Hot Line
1-800-HIT-HOME (1-800-448-4663)

For More Information

Useful Addresses

Association for Death Education and
Counseling (ADEC)
342 North Main Street
West Hartford, CT 06117-2507

Canadian Mental Health Association
2160 Yonge Street
Third Floor
Toronto, ON M4S 2Z3
CANADA
www.cmha.ca/english/homeng.htm
Makes referrals for all types of loss

The Compassionate Friends
PO Box 3696
Oak Brook, IL 60522-3696
www.compassionatefriends.org
Many publications on losing a brother or sister

Holistic Animal Consulting Center
29 Lyman Avenue
Staten Island, NY 10305

Teen Age Grief (TAG)
PO Box 220034
Newhall, CA 91322-0034
www.smartlink.net/~tag/info.html
Grief support for teens

For Further Reading

Fitzgerald, Helen. *The Grieving Teen: A Guide for Teenagers and Their Friends.*
New York: Simon and Schuster, 2000.

Hipp, Earl. *Help for the Hard Times: Getting Through Loss.* Center City, MN:
Hazelden, 1995.

Kuehn, Eileen. *Divorce: Finding a Place.* Mankato, MN: Capstone, 2001.

Kuehn, Eileen. *Death: Coping With the Pain.* Mankato, MN: Capstone, 2001.

Peacock, Judith. *Teen Suicide.* Mankato, MN: Capstone, 2000.

Glossary

accommodation (uh-kom-uh-DAY-shuhn)—the final phase of the grieving process; this is the slow acceptance of a loss on a day-to-day basis.

avoidance (uh-VOI-duhnss)—the first phase of the grieving process, in which a loss is not acknowledged

bereavement (buh-REEV-muhnt)—a feeling of shock and grief at someone's death

confrontation (kon-fruhn-TAY-shuhn)—the second phase of the grieving process, in which a person comes face-to-face with a loss

denial (di-NYE-uhl)—a refusal to accept that a loss has occurred

empathy (EM-puh-thee)—the ability to understand the experiences and feelings of other people

grief (GREEF)—emotions that go with mental suffering from a loss, such as sharp or painful sadness

grieving (GREE-ving)—the process of feeling and dealing with grief

post-traumatic stress disorder (POST-truh-MAT-ik STRESS diss-OR-dur)—feelings that occur long after a person has been exposed to violence

self-esteem (SELF-ess-TEEM)—a person's belief in the value of herself or himself

rite of passage (RITE uv PASS-ihj)—a ritual or ceremony to celebrate an occasion of growth and change

support group (suh-PORT GROOP)—a group of people who meet together to help each other with loss or other issues

survivor (sur-VYE-vur)—a person who lives after a person close to him or her has died

Index

Index